The Ones

Orange Rose Press
a division of Orange Rose Co
www.orangerose.co

ISBN: 979-8-9885364-1-3

Illustrations by Canva
Cover design by Amber Campbell

The Ones

Amber Campbell

ORANGE
ROSE
PRESS

For the one who didn't get to hold my first book.
Miss you, dad.

Love is as strong as you make it.
It can create an array of sunrises
Or leave a wake of destruction.
Sometimes you believe you chose a sunrise
Until the debris swirls around you.
Sometimes you're the eye of the storm,
And someone else is holding you down,
Preventing you from spreading pain
But receiving it all the same.
We never stop growing,
So forgive yourself,
And never forget the ones
You left,
The ones
Who left you,
And especially the ones
Who chose to stay.

Table of Contents

The Ones I Left   11

The Ones Who Left   53

The Ones Who Stayed   93

The Ones I Left

Dreaming

If I had a kiss for every time I dreamt of your touch,
I would know the softness of your lips as well as I
know the coldness of an empty bed.

Will you hold me in this moment?

No, that's too forward. You aren't mine to cherish. I
can love you, I can dream about you, I can fantasize
about us, but you are not my forever.

Right?

It's just a crush.

I'd rather regret not doing something than
comprehend the consequences that could hurt me.
But not all regret is bad.

Longing and daydreaming are just that. They don't
have to lead to missed opportunities, lost chances.
Maybe, instead, they're the one place I can speak
without backlash.

I will not dream of your touch, not out loud where
my words cannot be taken back.

Forbidden

I'm not supposed to touch you,
But if I could
I would run my fingertips over every inch of your
skin and map your tattoos like a trail to your soul.

I'm not supposed to kiss you,
But if I could
I would kiss every scar until you forgot all the pain
they inflicted.

I'm not supposed to hold you,
But if I could
I would cradle your body in my arms, rest your head
on my chest, and run my fingers through your hair
until you fell asleep.

I'm not supposed to caress you,
But if I could
I would soothe your body with gentle moans as
much as I would force every limb to tremble under
my tongue.

I'm not supposed to entrust you with my deepest
secrets,
But if I could
You would know as much about me as the tear-
stained pages in my nightstand.

I'm not supposed to want you,
But since I do
I will shower you with affection in every word,
action, and touch I give to you.

I'm not supposed to love you,
But I think I do.

Foretaste

I thought wrong.
I thought having a sliver
Of your love
Would sustain me and maintain me
But no.
The first kiss
Was a foretaste
Of everything I had been missing,
Of the love that once left me
Disgraced.
You opened a window
Where I saw a wall
And without demolishing
The tender heart inside
You opened my eyes
To a sight more wondrous
And more beautiful
Than the one standing before me.

I took a bite
And was swallowed whole.

Fun

Drunk on your words
And high on your touch
Got me cross faded
From too much love
I don't know what
            to do
                  besides
                       kiss you

Red

You know how they say that your first healthy relationship will have you thinking that you're a toxic person? That you're the one with all the red flags and warnings?

My dear, I say this with all the love mustered in a thousand galaxies: I will always be orange. It's my namesake. Based on statistics, if there is always one red flag, and mine is an amber wave of grain, it looks like you're fucked.

Philosophy

I'm not smart
In an intellectual sort of way
Where I can dissect the political theory
Of Friedrich and his revolutionary socialism
Or Karl and his manifesto of
Fancy words and political economy,
But I can sit with you
And drink a beer,
So long as you don't mind it's Irish.
You seem to lean toward German delicacies
That are far fancier than what I'm used to,
But you seem as comfortable in this dive bar
As I do,
Watching the screens
And eavesdropping on conversations,
Your shoulder touching mine
And nothing more.

But you like to hear me talk,
Even if it's not as intricately woven as
The men you surround your mind with.
And while I can't talk theories,
I can talk about kindness and justice,
And you let me ramble
As though I spoke to a crowd
Sparking a revolution,
Anarchy of the socialist decree!
Blazoning the vision of a manifesto
To overthrow the patriarchy!
But really it's just the Guinness,
And you're having a good time
With the nonsense it brings,
And I'm having a good time
Wondering what it all means
Until you finally decide to kiss me.

Cats

You're a really great guy
And I know we'll never last,
But I answer each time you message
Because a booty call means
I get to see your cats.

Alive

Do you know the pain
And confusion
Of questioning everything you've chosen
Or done?
To wonder if you've made all
The wrong choices
When everyone told you
How right they were?
They didn't know you.
You didn't know you,
Not yet.

But every word,
Every touch–
Every night I sleep
I dream of your face,
Of your hands,
Of your smile,
Of the most pain-staking heart
I've ever encountered,
And I want to put your pieces together
Not how they were, but how you need
Because you're not who you were,
And neither am I, but together
It's something new.

The world told me one thing,
But my heart said another,
And now my heart is with you.
You may strike it with lightning,
You may drown it in rain,
You may deafen in thunder,
And with that I have never felt more
Alive.

Rock

How dare you love me and leave.
How dare you teach me kindness
And rip it away like a thief in the night.
How dare you heal my wounds
And cut new ones in the same breath.
My blood soaks the ground,
My tears stain the trees.
My cries scream in the wind–
You cannot love me
And expect me to be okay after.
You can't be everything I prayed for
And then teach me to be wary of what I wish.

I dreamt of you,

Molded you in the deepest crevice of my heart,

And breathed you into life with my soul,

And you ended my everything with a kiss.

I loved you,

I love you still.

You are tempestuous and uncontrollable,

And I am steady and predictable.

When your wanderlust has faded,

And you're ready to embrace the constant that is me,

I will be your rock.

Lights

I want to drive with you
And look at Christmas lights.
We can listen to country music
And Nickelback,
And I'll probably sneak in
Taylor Swift.
But I'll bring hot chocolate
And you'll bring the sparkle to my eyes.

Art

I've always wished
I could draw instead of write.
It seems easier to convey love and hope
Into colors and shapes
Than in letters and commas that never quite
      Sound
            like what
                  I want.
But you smile and say my words are beautiful
And I'm reminded
      Colors and shapes aren't art until
someone sees them for their intent,
And you saw my poorly worded intentions
Of affection and gratitude as masterpieces,
      And I'm speechless
inside the veil of pastel hues
that envelope all that is you.

Gentle

Be gentle with my heart
Because Lord knows
I'm not.

Woman

Heaven taught me to fear Our Father,
But Hell warned me of a woman's anger.
While I still believe in Jesus,
Knowing I am something the Devil fears
Fills me with more power
Than my earthly father
Could ever harness.

Cheat

I can see
Why she wished it were someone else
She was waking up with
Now that I've woken up
To a face as revolting
As the one who dared to call me
By her name
Just like she
Called you
His.

Moon

I'll keep this short and sweet
Like you kept us.
I always wanted a man
To give me the moon,
And you did,
But you also took the moon away
And taught me a valuable lesson:
If a man says he doesn't love his ex
Before he says he loves you,
He never loved you,
And he never stopped loving her.
May the moon rise above
The despicable hill
From which she was created
To see you for what you are.

Barfolk

If you knew me when my father was alive,
You don't know me now.
Don't hug me like we're old friends.
Don't ask me how I'm doing like you care.
Don't look my husband up and down
At my dead dad's memorial.
Once a cheater, always a cheater.
Don't make a side dish the main course,
But you already knew that.

That's what the rest of the barfolk told you,
But they have no integrity
Because their allegiance is to whoever has the most
Money to spend on alcohol
Because none of your friends are sober,
But you already knew that.

They'll stab you in the back
Like you did me,
And I hope you remember the way my father yelled
And how pathetic you both are
For making me feel so small.
You're no better than all the women
Who have ever hurt you because now I know:
You don't how to love
Without abusing someone,
But you already knew that.

Superhero

I wish I could move on
And forget you existed,
But your name chills my soul
The same way it did
Six years ago
When you misled me.
I trusted you,
A child to a man,
But I wasn't a child to you, was I?
You'd been with younger than me,
So I was a little ripe for your tongue
And my bitterness turned you out
Because I wanted you to be better,
Not knowing that this was the best
You had ever been.

A shell of a man
Would be harder than you.
A coward with a dream
To run and hide overseas
And never again see your child
Because it's hard being a father,
And you regret it,
But you won't speak of it.
You burdened me with your deepest regrets,
And I promised to never speak them out loud
For as long as I lived.
Aren't you pleased to see
That I never did?

You may have thought of yourself as a hero
For doing what was hard for you,
So allow me to introduce myself.
I am the Hubris you overlooked.
When you thought you had a friend,
I was collecting pieces of your heart
To show the world your true colors
Because I never needed to seek revenge
Until you taught me how,
Using my innocence
To earn back a life
You hated.

I hope you're happy
Because you don't deserve it,
And soon your daughter will see you
For the evil you are.
Once she learns that you wanted to leave,
I hope she reminds you
Of all the happy endings she could've had
If only you hadn't sacrificed me.

Monster

Running your hands through my hair,
Feeling your lips on my skin.
Forgetting when you promised me every sin
As long as we didn't speak the word affair.
My fragile heart in your hands, beyond repair
But beholden to your touch
As though your shallow love could ever be enough
Without a semi-hopeful prayer.
Toss me to the lions
That crowd your favorite bar.
Say my eyes twinkle like stars
That always seemed so far.
Where have you been?
Now that I bury my body in the dirt,
Now that I hide this hurt while you shirked
All the responsibility of letting me in.
I wish I could shed the regret
Of lying in your bed,
Your name always a bad taste
I can't seem to swallow.
I love you, you said.
Tell the truth, I begged.
It'd be easier to lose you if you were dead
Instead of in her bed.

Villain

I took your heart,
Piece by piece,
And put it back together
And carried on my way,
Knowing it would shatter
But sending up a prayer
That I used enough glue
To stop it from bleeding out
Like it did when I met you.
You trusted me to fix it
But also trusted I would stay.
I should have better explained
That I can only heal
As often as I break.
I always have the best intentions,
But my actions don't know them.
It's not your fault
I changed direction.

Fog

I can't see what's in front of my nose.
Knowing the truth doesn't ease
The monsters that erupt when you speak
Because I believed you when you showed me
All the ways you would hurt me,
And I believed I could help you,
No–
Believed I could change you,
Transform you into a person you would be proud of,
Not understanding how proud you were
Of rising from your ashes,
Of overcoming your struggles,
Of standing again when the others kicked you
When you were down.

I thought you needed my help
When what you needed was me by your side,
Giving you rest and understanding your pain
Even though I had never felt this type of pain
Before I met you
And witnessed firsthand what pain did to someone
Who wasn't like me.
I was told to brush it off and walk it off,
And you told yourself the lessons I learned
Because you didn't have someone looking out for you.
Even with the bottle in his hand,
I saw the love my father had for me,
While you looked from the ground
At the man who shoved you down,
And to this day all you can see
Is the rage in his eyes,
And all my bruised heart and fragile soul can do
Is cry tears you never meant to produce.

Your life was a fog but my eyes glowed brighter
Than the moon on a clear night
Because the truth was in your arms
And not on their lips,
And the expectations clouded my sight
Until I wandered blind in the murky waters,
Until you pulled me out from under.
Your truth lit up the path,
Iridescent in the mud,
And the fog was never what you did
But only what everyone else said.

I know you forgave me for when I mistook your tears
For those of sorrow and not relief,
But will you forgive me again
When I project my insecurities onto you
And expect you to fix me
Like I failed to fix you?

Darker

My thoughts race with the image
Of your hands interlaced in my hair
And your breath on my lips,
And I think I can taste
The cigarettes on your tongue
Even though I've never been close enough
To know what it feels like
When you fall asleep in my arms
Because you're my wildest fantasy.
You're the light at the end of my tunnel,
Yet the more I move forward,
The dimmer you shine
Because you're not mine to love,
And I hate the universe for bringing you
To me
When all it did was yank me away
And ask,
See what could have been?

You won't believe me
When I say this makes sense
Because I only look good on paper
And against your body pinned to the wall
With my demons and monsters licking the air
That you breathe in my existence,
As though I could ever be deserving
Of the one standing before me,
But I feed my flaws like a starving child
And they will never feel the satisfaction
Of enough,
Just like you would never feel the wholeness of
My love.

I am wanted by everyone
But needed by no one,
And all I want
Is to need someone the way you
Need the sunlight to kiss your cheeks
And the snow to warm your soul
Because you are one with the earth,
And I am the epitome of humanity's sins.
The gold you see enveloping me
Is tarnished underneath,
And the silver wound through my hair
Leaves a seasick green in its wake.

I am the perfect woman for you,
So long as my darkest desires taste the light
Emanating from your soft heart
And feed from you until you're as damaged
As the lovers before you.
I want to take it back
So you never know a life
With me in it
Because I know you were happier
When you believed your love was still out there,
And not at home writing poetry for eyes
That will never see it.

Spiral

Loving you is a rush,
But I'm scared of the high.
I get addicted to addicts
To end up out of their sight.
I know we don't see eye to eye,
But if you hold me tonight,
I promise to give you
Every tainted piece
Of this diseased heart.

I can't kill myself to save you,
Not when you didn't know you were dying,
And not when you wouldn't
Have known I was gone
Until after you felt worthy
Of being with me.

The Ones Who Left

What doesn't kill us
Will wear us down
Until we wished it had.

Eclipse

Never mind, I changed
My mind.
Our parting was mutual.
I was unhappy you were cheating,
And you were cheating because I
Was too good to
Your daughter
And too good to you,
And that much wholeness
Couldn't fit in your shattered
Shell of a life,
So you darkened mine
Until I suffocated.
You tarnished my name
To revive the name of the one
Who cheated on you
With a man you entrusted
Like I trusted you.

You don't realize all the negativity you battle
Is invited into your home
Each time you chase away her shadows,
But she never loved you.
She never will.
She used you
Like you used me,
But instead of succumbing to the eclipse,
I stayed below ground
And reemerged with the sun
While you hid behind closed doors
With her.
Each time I encounter you in my new life,
I hope my light blinds you
Back into the cave she keeps you
So you never know the taste
Of unconditional love again.
You are woven of the same fabric:
Both gaslighters,
Both abusers,
Both cheaters,
Both eclipsing each other
Into ghosts everyone forgot
Ever existed.

Trapped

I built a haven.
Watched the walls rise,
The door hinge,
And the roof patch,
But now it is not mine.
I crafted a safe place
From planks of wood and squares of linoleum,
And now it traps me,
A comely jail cell reminding me
Of my brash decisions
And people-pleasing crutch.
I should have said something,
and I didn't,
And we both fell apart.
I tried to soften the blow,
But it only made things worse.
I am trapped by the yellowed walls
That once showered me in a snowy oasis
And the rusted doorknobs
That once led to wondrous adventures
Without leaving a reddish stain
On my fingertips.

Only the car
With its engine and tires
Helps me escape.
But I don't get far
Before you call and ask,
When are you coming back?
I'm not.
But I don't say this
Because I will return,
Because I can't anger you,
Because of the people-pleasing crutch I got
From my dad.
I'm scared of angry men,
So I invite them into my safe places
And am trapped until
They are done with me.

Fear

I fear the men,
Even the ones who protect me
Because I know yelling leads to crying,
And the man responsible for my fear
Isn't alive to answer for his crimes.
And we read about crimes of passion,
But what about crimes of love?
A father's love is only as deep
As his darkest scar.

Senses

You brought me to the corridor of the student union
under the starless night sky.

I had a ring in my pocket.
You had a bad taste in your mouth.

You said you'd love me for all time,
But my watch ran slower than yours.

You said I was the greatest woman you'd ever been
with. What a shame you weren't the only man I'd
had.

You said all the pretty speeches in all the pretty
clothes, but your hands were hidden behind your
back until you pulled me in close enough to leave
the knife.

Because I listened when I should have seen. I let you
touch me until I couldn't smell the sour aroma of
bullshit.

You puppeteered my senses until I couldn't taste her
on your lips until you asked me how I liked it.

Vesper

I never think of you
When I'm sober.
Something about the
Bitter, nutty flavor on my
Tongue reminds my brain
That you exist, my heart
That you aren't here, my mouth
That I once dared to
Grace your ears with
I Love You.
I often say of all my exes
There is only one I don't want
To punch in the face, and you
Aren't him.

In fact, you've won the top spot
On my list of men
Who could bring my father back
From the grave to meet
Your teeth with knuckles.
I never think of you
When I'm sober,
But I curse your name
With each swallow of Guinness
That warms my soul in a way you
Never could.

Littles

I have loved you greater than any heart could muster. Only a few knew of you, but even they couldn't know how much I loved you. How much I was ready to give my life for you. How much I would fight to hold you now. How much grief your father held back so I could heal. How much I hid from him when I could no longer bear for another to see the pain.

No one will compare to you. February 17th will forever be your day. There hasn't been one since you. Maybe there won't be. You might be my one and only. I tried to fill the void with animals, and it helps. Others find alternative measures, but I'm not strong enough for the injections and the doctor visits. If you send me another, thank you. If you don't, then all my love will belong to you alone.

Your father misses you all the time. I'm sorry you never met your grandpa, but at least he's with you now. You would have loved the puppies. Your grandma bought outfits she wanted to dress you in. I'm writing again. It's been six and a half years, but I'm writing, and it's to write about the child I never held.

I felt you pass when it happened. You weren't even formed yet, but I knew. Nothing to save. Nothing to help. You didn't have my eyes or your father's nose or a heart for my body to feel beating. But you were loved. So loved, my child. Everyone wanted you. Everyone waited for you. Everyone wanted to hold you. But in the end only I did. Not in my arms, but in my body. I knew you were there. I knew you were mine.

I thought I would be okay as a stepmom. I thought I only wanted to love a child, to give them love and care and that would be enough. But you ruined me, little one. You made me realize how much I wanted you but couldn't have you. May you fly high and rest with all the family we've laid to rest since you've been gone. I love you.

Cardinal

From outside my window, the cardinal watched the
leaves rustle in the breeze and eyed my dog on the
ground eyeing it and the two are locked in a battle of
freeze tag where tag means death and so the cardinal
perches on the branch and only his pupils dance
across the yard.

The redness of his wings matches the redness of the
dress that hangs in a thick glass case on the living
room, and I tell everyone the fabric of the dress was
brought over on the Mayflower just like you told me
and like your grandmother told you and whose
grandmother told her because we come from a long
line of prideful Yankees of Pennsylvania even
though no one in Oil City knows of us any more
than the world knows of Oil City, Pennsylvania.

And then I remember the story of your childhood
friend who threw a lit match down her family's well
when you were barely ten and it caught fire at the
bottom because of how much gas was in the well
and decades later when you showed me obituaries of
those you've lost it will strike you as epiphanic
when I ask if the oil in the water lines is what caused
all the cancer that took your friends.

You made plenty of friends wherever you went, from Pennsylvania to Carolina to El Paso where you laid to rest among the mountains you knew in your heart were shaped by God because nothing that beautiful is ever human made and you would toss out every green inch of your home state if it meant always seeing the clear blue skies and muddy brown mountains of West Texas.

And the dog barks and the cardinal flies and I'm brought back to the moment but I linger as long as I can because getting lost in stories without endings and beginnings are the only way I know to be with you because it was the only way I was with you when you were here and we never had a cardinal in our yard for every spring and every autumn until you passed and gave him to us so we would never forget you.

Your time with us ended, but your legacy continues with every long-winded story that occupies my mind and draws me out of the moment but somehow keeps me in a moment, like a portal I can't open or close but still have access whenever you deem it and I guess that's what heaven is for me if it lets me still have you.

Garden

The ivy clung to the wood
Paneling the house,
And I watched it soar
Into the sky.
I pictured an Irish castle
Overgrown with green leaves and vines,
A quaint secret garden
To call yours and mine.
My father said to be wary
Of the ivy
Because it chokes and kills
And damages the frame.
I protected the growth for what is was
And loved it all the same.
But then you left,
And the ivy soared,
And it wrapped around the stems
Of the rose garden I planted
Before you came along.

It took some years before I understood
That the ivy was suffocating
The yellow and pink buds,
My sweet, velvety loves,
And even in death my father's always right.
I tore the ivy off, ripping each leaf
As I wrenched my roses free,
And the thorns nipped me less ferociously
As their nonexistent buds salted the air,
Stale and bare.
The ivy lay strewn across the garden,
Browning before my eyes.
How naive of me to believe
That something beautiful could be unwaveringly kind.
The roses may have stung me,
But they flourished me in grace afterwards,
And now I know not to seek beauty
Before I accept the pain.

Phantoms

I'm on top of the world
But terrified to look down
Because I know that despite my hope,
I'm closer than I realize to the ground.
I dream of the past,
Pretend it's the present,
And ruin my future
Before it becomes what it's meant.
Each night I pray
To find solace in the arms
Of those whose hearts are lawless.
I'm so in love with love
That I mistake it for truth
Until it loses the mask,
And the once adoration no longer soothes.

Advice

Hey,
It's been a while.
I hope you're happy
And doing whatever it is
Dead people do.
I miss you a lot right now.
All the time really,
But especially now.
I want to ask you if I'm doing
Everything right
Even though you always told me
Choose my path and hold conviction,
But you were also here
To remind me
That you loved me
No matter what I chose,
And now I have to remind myself,
And I'm bad at that
Because that involves self-motivation,
And I am the generation
Who realized our faults
Before our potential
Even though they gave us
Participation trophies,
Which made us feel smaller.

Perhaps that's why
I seek out your advice
Even though I know the answer,
And that the answer would be silence
Like when you were here
Because I never wanted to upset you.
I don't regret any of my decisions,
And that would make you proud,
Even though my decisions revolved
Around the amount of liquid courage
Coursing through your system
Or the mountain of regret you carried
After your mother died,
And I told you like you told me
Hundreds of times before
That she loved you,
She was proud of you,
And it makes me angry to realize
That I, your child,
Had to tell you these things
And tell them often
Because when you were young,
You rarely heard them.

Even in your drunken nights
I never doubted your love for me
Because you reminded me each day
That I was your greatest accomplishment.
So maybe I don't need to ask you
About the problems on my mind
Because we both know I'll figure it out
And celebrate with you after,
And despite the fear my inner child still feels,
My adult mind and heart empathize.
So I pour a glass of whiskey for you,
Knowing it wasn't the whiskey that made you bad,
But the hand life dealt you,
And the lack of advice you had
Until we found each other
And created our own little world.

Sad

I'm sorry I made you cry
When I read my words out loud,
But please don't worry
Because I'm learning
That I write sad poetry
Because I like how your face scrunches
And your eyes water
And know that even without
My skin touching yours,
I can change your whole perspective
And ruin your day
In the best way
Because I'm a writer,
And my happiness derides
From the tears you cry
When my words blend and merge and transform
Into a world you believe is yours.
My dear,
All of it is.

Phase

I know you think
I'll leave
Because you're a phase,
But I fear
You'll leave
Because I'm a new notch.
We are the same.

Summer

The colors in your eyes
Were as bright
As the fire
Of your sign,
And I believe
In constellations and stars
If it means
Believing in you.
A reckless season,
A flash of sheets and wildflowers,
Bluebonnet fields like a sea
In the wilderness of West Texas,
And your eyes melted my soul
Like the heat of the sun burned my skin,
Like how you burned
My soul and cursed me to a life
Where I chase every bloom in summer
And caress its stem,
But leave it rooted
Because taking from the earth
Would be taking from you,
And I took enough from you
That summer.

Apology

I'm sorry I couldn't be
What you wanted
Or who you thought I was.
Maybe that's on me,
For knowing the way I say
Words to make them sound
Like velvety rose petals on your
Skin and how I induce the shudder your
Shoulders make when your
Breath hitches and you can't
Look me in the eye
Because you know I wasn't your forever.
But I hope I changed your
Expectations and raised the
Standard for every future lover who
Embraces the warmth of your
Heart and the sweetness of your
Soul and I hope they erase every
Scent I left on your body.

Forgiveness

I still feel the tears
That trailed down my cheeks
The night I lost you.
The pain that racked my body,
The shaking that wouldn't stop,
The sweat that chilled my bones,
Staring at the blood clot in the toilet
And knowing it was
You.

Eleven weeks in my womb
For eleven seconds in dirty water
That I didn't have in my heart to flush
And instead stared at you,
Wondering what might have been
If your heart ever formed.
If you'd have your father's kindness
And my careful scrutiny,
But then the water flowed down
Down
Down
Until you were gone
From
Me.

I still think about you
When the pain gets too intense,
And I flash back to that night
When my muscles contorted and convulsed.
A labor meant only for expulsion
When it should have been life,
But then I wonder if
Everything
I've since built
Would have been built
If I was cradling you
Right now.

I found my voice again.
The words that once eluded my grasp,
Danced across my tongue,
And flitted through my fingertips like wisps
Now flood the pages before me.
They would be stained red
If not for the skin between me and the ink,
And I am torn between wishing I held you
And grateful I can speak.

I hope you forgive me
For being happy
And finding purpose
Without you.
They say women are more than mothers,
But fuck.
That's all I wanted to be.
I wanted to be your mom
And hold you when you slept
And hold you when you cried
And hold you when the world felt too bright
For the overly kind soul
That would have been produced
From two people who are too kind themselves.

I finally understood
How my father must have felt
To feel so insecure and inadequate
In my anxieties and trouble
And knowing a small child would rely on me,
But they wouldn't know of these
Adult predicaments.
They would have held my hand
Before crossing the street
And thought my arms
Would always keep them safe,
And I hope his arms
Are keeping you safe
Now that you've finally met
Your grandpa.

I don't think I would have survived
The whirlwind that would have been
My dad and his new best friend.

Questions

I thought I could see the future
But I mistook it for the present again,
Forgetting one ends
And the other never begins.

It's easy for others to love me,
But it's hard for me to love in return.
Either I fall so quickly I lose interest,
Or I fall slowly and see the flaws,
And I learned best to abandon ship
Before I tangle the lines and drown us both.
I cannot love without leaving an emotional mess
Of muddled feelings and wounded hope,
And I turn my back on friends and family
Because I don't love based on
Title or blood or proximity
But on what I need,
And if I don't need you–

I wish I could see into the future
And know how my heart will operate
After spending all my time with my love,
To provide him the answers he asks in my head.
Yes, I love you still.
Yes, I want only you.
Yes, I'm glad I chose you.
But did he choose me,
Or did he fall into me because of how
Easy it was to love me,
to trust and be vulnerable?
The whole time you're healing,
I'm vanishing into the fog
Of failed memories and lost feelings
Wondering if this is it,
And if I'm still breathing.

Air
In
Air
Out

I weave my fingers through locks of hair
That has your scent all over them,
But then you're covered in my smell,
And I don't know where you end and I begin and
Everything cascades into a snowball
Of love and want and hope,
And I love that you hope for us
And that you only want for me
And that I can say the same
Without a hiccup in my breath
Or a lie in my heart.

To the ones I've loved,
I wish I knew how to help,
To heal your wounds I opened,
To beg for forgiveness I'll never ask.
I'm not even sure I want it.
I have what my heart needs
In the people who protected me
Time and time again,
And maybe that's how I'm loved
To give love.
It's not about exchanges and transactions
But who carried the umbrella
Over my head
When everyone else
Tried to share.

You still cross my mind from time to time,
But my heart no longer sighs,
And my soul remembers what once was,
But my fingers forgot the touch.
The memories that we once swore were
masterpieces,
True works of art,
Are but shadows against a fog.
I can see the trace of your body,
But it's merely a mirage,
A darkened oasis of when you were once
Enough.

And if you ask the question
Of if I'm doing well,
I'll always say yes.
I expect nothing less
When I ask in return
Because our truths are hidden beneath the lies
I now tell to you,
Because these lies are meant to protect
From the truths we've lost and learned.

My muse is my love,
But my love is not my muse.

The Ones Who Stayed

You can't heal without love,
But you can love
Without healing,
And those are the ones
I left
Because they weren't
You.

Vulnerable

It's hard to take blame,
But I can't blame you for the truth
Anymore than you can blame me
For the emergence of the reality
That we're not perfect,
That we're still learning to communicate,
That our words come together
In a wave of silk in our minds
And self-destruct into a pile of garbage
When we open our mouths.
You warned me about your works in progress,
But I was so engulfed in hiding my flaws
That you didn't get the same porcelain caution,
And the whirlwind of crushed spirits
And empty hands
Doesn't recognize good intent from the bad.

Hurt hearts only know two things:
Forgiveness and revenge,
And I tried both and failed both
Because my heart was in the wrong
Each time.
Each stumble from me was a criticism on you,
And every slip from you was a reprimand on me,
And we dug holes so deep
We breathed in dirt like air.
Instead of sharing the fault we compared
Who's fuck-ups was greater and widened the chasm
That pushed us apart in a rotten ensnare.
But then we tossed the shovels,
Found footholds in the rock we formed between
ourselves.
We chipped away at the insecurities,
The fears,
The words we can't take back,
And the words we're still learning to say.
You can't blame the pain that made me
invulnerable,
But I can blame my reaction
When you try to open me up
And hold my heart the way
You always wanted someone
To hold yours.

Raccoon

Everyone before you
Gave me nicknames based on
What I told them about me,
And they fit me into the box
I told them to.
But you paid no heed
To what I claimed to be
And instead showed me
My truth and how it looked to you.
My truth is a trash panda:
Chubby cheeked,
Clumsy as hell,
Constantly searching
For food we don't have
Because healthy me
Went grocery shopping
With my grabby hands
That grab you at all hours of the day
Even when you're not in the mood.
You're a timid little hedgehog,
And I am the rambunctious raccoon,
Egging you to play.

1,124

We confuse love with movies
And honeymoons and highlight reels,
When it's also the everyday,
And big fights and the mundane.
Love will not last
If it cannot survive
The most basic of human routines.
I questioned if my
Love could survive,
But 1,124 days
And you're still here,
Wanting me,
Loving me,
Pulling your hair out
At my constant questioning
Of myself and of us,
And you hold me and scold me
For doubting myself and us.
I wonder how love can be this strong,
Can last through the years and months
And nights of loneliness.

I know to know my worth,
But I've been cast aside
By others before you,
Others whose whispers
Lick my ears with their scarlet intent:
I'm not wife material.
I'm not mature enough.
I'll be great for
Someone else one day.
I'm not their *one*.
I'm unbelievable and unwanted.
How then can I believe you
When you say you want me
When everyone else so easily believed
They would find better?
You thought you were the difficult partner,
And yet my insecurities and trauma
Give your problems a fair fight
In the metaphorical boxing ring
Our government calls marriage,
Where both sides punch themselves
To see who will win
By losing first.

But you stop my fist
From flying into my nose
And breaking the delicate button
That you love to kiss,
That you tap with your fingertip
When you're half asleep
And can't see me in the dark.
You protect me from myself
When I am the only one
Deserving of the wrath
That I give unto myself.
1,124 days
Of fighting ourselves
To preserve the other
Until I clung to the cliff's edge
Ready to drop and soar
Into the clouds and feel the wind
On my face as airy and warm and safe
As your breath when you lean down and
Kiss me,
And say,
"I love you,
Now go to sleep."

ADHD

Until I met you I had no idea what ADHD really
was.
Inattentive
      Hyper
           Loud
                Chatty
But it had nothing to do with the reality
Of learning the complete history
Of bananas at 10:17 pm on a Wednesday
When you stumbled into a fixation
After getting bored with your
Submarines and how they're evil video
But the bananas were genetically altered
And in fact bananas don't look like
How we know them now
And they were infected with a fungus
That almost wiped them out
That I thought was due to a shortage
in one of the World Wars
And that's why Hostess changed
The Twinkie cream flavor
From banana to vanilla

But you said my dad was wrong and that's okay
Because he's not here to argue with you
But the fungus wiped out the–was it Catherine?
I don't remember the name
But it left us with Cavendish bananas
And that's what we eat now
But because they're modified
They'll probably be extinct soon
I said that's fine since I'm allergic now
And you said, yeah, that's what I thought too.
And then I fell asleep and dreamt of a submarine
Filled with bananas of every variety I couldn't name
But the submarine had a face
and it was chasing me from inside itself
And it wasn't until I woke up sweating
That I realized
I still had no idea why submarines are bad.

Healing

I tried to find love in others before you.
I gave them my heart and trusted them
With secrets, inner hopes, and hidden fears,
And they thanked me for my time
And used what I taught them
To give love to others.
It took me too many years to learn
That you can't heal without love,
But you can love
Without healing,
And those are the ones
I left
Because they weren't
You.

I gave away the love I had,
But it was the same love each time,
Just repurposed in pretty new paper.
And then I met you,
And the love you receive is the love that gathered dust
In a delicate box I hid in the closet.
The love you receive is desperate
Only for the love you give.
You allow me to be me
And still be yours.
We healed ourselves
Instead of healing each other,
And it's for that reason
That we endured.

Fighting

Sometimes I pick fights with you so I can remember
the anger that protected me for so long, and I feel
guilty for forcing your hand, for dragging you into
the arena of my fucked-up brain. But you mediate
my fury with soft-spoken words and rationality
when all I wanted was screaming and tears. You
never give me what I want.

Except when you gave me you.

Contained

Dad always told me,
"Don't fall in love so hard, so fast.
Date, get to know someone,
Don't fall in love with each one."
He was right,
About the part where I don't fall in love with each one,
But I can't withhold love.
I can't contain my love.
So I found someone who can't contain theirs,
And we built a home out of too much, too soon
And drown in kisses and overuse
Of those three words that terrify everyone.
It's better than suffocating under the weight
Of never letting someone in or from the smoke
Of false pretenses and social masks of acceptance,
And when you called my dad to ask
For my hand, he told you,
"It doesn't matter what I think.
She's an adult. It's her choice."
And he was right about that, too.

Everyday

We were in high school.
You texted me in February.

"Happy Valentine's Day! You're my valentine."

I responded,

"Happy Valentine's Day! You're my everyday."

And that is how every man
You will ever meet
Will fail to reach the expectations
That were impossibly raised by me.

Coyote

The irony of my favorite loved ones
Being compared to animals
Is not lost on me.
Your poor Indian name butchered
By hundreds of white tongues
Until they managed to rhyme it with coyote,
A name that has 1.25 syllables,
And we gave it three,
And for that I'm sorry.
But thank you for still being here.
Nineteen years of friendship,
Eighteen years of thinking
You're a nut job,
And seventeen years of you wondering
Why the hell you've kept me around.
Well, it's because I know how to drive
And not plow through curb stoppers
Like speed bumps,
And I remind you the world doesn't revolve around
You
Because as we both know it revolves around
Me.
But despite your horrible driving
And mispronounced name,
There is no one on this earth I would rather
Enjoy saag paneer and aloo paratha with than you.
Thanks boo.

Sam

It's hard being the protagonist when you're in the spotlight. So kind, so wise, so unequivocally annoying in how you're always right. I've come a long way since we met (600 miles to be precise), but each day I strive to become the person I was when we first met.

Joyful, ambitious, prepared to conquer the world. I used to love the challenges; now I hide under the covers. You walked me through so many firsts: boyfriend, college, big girl job, and break-up. My faith was there but so much has changed. There's nothing you could have done, and tell your mom as much. Don't forget to tell her I love her because I know my name is still in her prayers.

You never abandoned me, even with months of no contact. I never abandoned you because we both know boys suck. Your first time leaving the country was with me, and your next will be, too. Before you ask, no, I don't know the date of the next cruise.

You got me through my darkest moments. You're still getting me through. You're going to make a fantastic nurse, but you'll never be as good as the good friend you are to me. But you might be, because you're the best.

I love you more than words can express. Be strong, be peaceful, be all you want to be, but promise you'll never be a stranger in my memory.

Pocahontas

When you were little, you grew your hair out so long you looked like Pocahontas. It went past your waist, and you refused to cut it for years. It was beautiful, but it protected you.

Maybe if you cover your face, men won't notice you. Maybe if they have to slay a jungle-lush of ponytails and braids they won't bother you. But we all know how maybes work.

You've spent enough time hiding your body and your truth. Pull your hair out of your face and feel the salty air on your arms and the sun's warmth on your burning cheeks. Embrace nature in the way you should have been embraced. Give love so majestically the memories of regrets wash away.

I'm not telling you to forgive. It's why I'm a bad Christian. You'd argue that's because you're Protestant and I'm Catholic, but it goes beyond that. I never forgive. My brain forgets everything, so my heart burdens the pain that stays when forgiveness is withheld, and I live my truth.

Be greater than I allow myself to be. Run to every corner of the world with me, and I will provide the safety you've rarely known. Be free. Be joyful. Sing whatever song the princess in you calls forth. I'll forever be the best friend who plays the drums to your melody.

MOH

You asked me to be your maid of honor,
And I asked if I could think about it.
You said sure and reached for the gifted jewelry, but
I withheld it.
You laughed and rolled your eyes at me.
If it means keeping the shiny necklace,
I'll be your maid of honor.
I guess nineteen years of friendship
Requires *some* responsibility.

Wealthy

Growing up, I wanted a red brick house.
Something with a foundation,
Something that didn't require faucets dripping
When the cold front blew in,
Something that couldn't be repossessed
Like the blue Geo Metro we owned, or was it the red?
I never brought friends over
Because I didn't want them to know
Just how poor we really were,
Not living in a house.
Now that I'm the age you were
When we lived in that mobile home,
I realized we never needed coins
To take to the lavandería
That all the pregnant white girls at my high school
Wanted to name their daughters
Because they thought it meant lavender.

We didn't have expenses to go on
Extravagant vacations or Disney World,
But you taught me money management,
A course still not taught in school
Because then more of us break out of
Generational curses, and the government
Can't have that if it wants to maintain
A 1% instead of a 99% wealth.
Because of learning from your mistakes,
I now take yearly vacations
Beyond my backyard,
And my dream trip to Ireland
Is no longer a dream.
It's all because you let me in,
To watch you cut coupons
And budget and sacrifice,
So that I could live my dream as an adult,
Not realizing that my childhood dreams
Would be outgrown by the time I was 17.

We didn't have the red brick house,
And I don't have one now,
But I have a tiny house on your land
That I can pay off in 10 years,
And it will be mine,
And no one will repossess it.
It doesn't have a cement foundation
But it has the family bones that you taught me
Are far more important.

Beaches

The sunshine kissing your cheeks,
The sand rubbing your toes,
The breeze brushing your hair,
The salt flavoring your soul:
The beach was made for you, my love.
If I only do one thing in this life,
It will be to take you to the ocean
Every day of your life
Until you feel my father
And my grandmother
Hugging you in the waves.
Always with you,
Always shining on you,
Like midday on the beach.

Genetics

I know the need of the alcoholic as well I know the clarity of the sober. I understand the plight of the user as well as I understand the ease of the clean. I'm caught between doing what's right and what's wrong but I don't know which is which. What if the same DNA asking what if, is the only thing holding me back?

Mine

You always told me I can't pour from an empty cup, but you forgot to teach me how to fill it up. So I found a broken person from who to take the droplets running through their cracks, but it was never enough. I thirsted for the love that wasn't in myself and ended up begging for breadcrumbs.

I give to everyone. It's yours, yours, yours. My heart, my soul, my love, my promises that are softer than paper and already torn. My words hold no weight because I weighed them down with nothings, and I emptied all I had before I left your nest with premature wings.

And my dad told me to be kind, but you hardened, didn't you? You let him and the world break down the kindness in your heart. You allowed men to come in and tell you how to be and stopped the course before you reached the breakthrough. So I watched you, and did the same, and I let men and women have all of the pieces of my heart just to watch them shatter it into a few more shards.

There are two halves to my soul, and half is you, but it's the worst half, the half that is bitter and angry. The other half is him, but it's the worst half, the half that is anxious and short-tempered. And the amalgamation of a functioning person I present to the world must be bubbly, patient, and calm. The mask has been worn so long that it comes up of its own accord, and I fade into the background as my socially acceptable presets play the part.

I desperately want something that is mine. Something that will nourish me and fill my cup when I've poured it out for yet another lonely traveler. I think I've found it, and for the first time in my life, it doesn't control me. It ebbs and flows with me, it cherishes the anger as much as the happy, and it celebrates the darkest parts of me in the brightest light I've ever produced.

I will forever be your rock, but I must be free as the wind for my soul. Like a tornado, I will ground myself when I am needed, but will soar into the clouds once the mask slips off, once the lights turn off, once the world has decided it needs just one more drop.

For fourteen years, I wrote stories, poems, songs, scripts, and everything in between. I wrote fervently, as though if I stopped for a day, I would lose the power to form words into sentences into a tale. Then, I spent seven years not writing, assuming the gift had been taken away, that my only dream from ages 10 to 24 was a fluke.

My entire childhood, I was The Writer. It frustrated me when no one could think of another adjective for me, but the truth is there were adjectives told about me in the seven years of unwritten truths that I didn't realize echoed the writerly traits I tried so hard to brush off: creative, intuitive, kind, intelligent, sarcastic, bubbly. These attributes brought back memories of characters I created and more than likely tortured emotionally, of battles waged on school grounds, of emotions I allowed to flow and release instead of now when I bottle them up because I forget how to communicate, even though I once took apart my mind down to the nuts and bolts and executed my thoughts as flawlessly as German engineering.

I gave up words, but they found their way back to me. I gave them away, and they insisted on being loved. Being known as The Writer wasn't a crutch, but a grace that I clumsily denied but even more clumsily accepted, vomiting words onto the page in a delirious panic as though I'll forget how to string them together. But the words don't forget. The words are eternal. The words are mine, and they are here to stay.

Thank you for reading. Please leave a review if you feel so inclined, and you can follow me on Instagram and YouTube (@OrangeRoseEdits) for all updates on my upcoming releases.

I hope you spread kindness to all you meet today. Forgiveness is optional and at your leisure.